Second Lieutenant. George S. Patton. Jr.
prepares equipment for saber exercises..
More photos and illustrations inside.

*"This instruction in the troops has for its object
to develop by means of the gymnastic
game of fencing, the desire and ability to
thrust and thrust accurately in battle."*

George S. Patton, Jr.,
Diary of the Instructor in Swordsmanship

Mounted Service School Press, 1915

Reprinted by

Dale Street Books

Silver Spring, Maryland

DIARY OF THE INSTRUCTOR IN SWORDSMANSHIP

At the Mounted Service School
Fort Riley, Kansas
1914-1915

By
George S. Patton, Jr.

To The Reader

World War II General George S. Patton, Jr. wrote *Diary of the Instructor in Swordsmanship* in 1915 while he was still a young lieutenant and fencing instructor at the Mounted Service School in Fort Riley, Kansas. It is reprinted here in its entirety, including all original photographs and graphics. This rare publication might have been lost to history but for the preservation efforts of the U.S. Army Heritage and Education Center in Carlisle, Pennsylvania.

Before his assignment to the Mounted Service School, Patton had already proven his expertise in the art of fencing by placing fifth in the Pentathlon at the 1912 Summer Olympics in Sweden. He next traveled to Saumur, France to study with M. L'Adjutant Clery, reputed to be the finest fencing master in Europe. After Patton returned to the States he invented the Patton Saber, a design so simple yet revolutionary, the War Department ordered 20,000 in 1913. He was then assigned to the Mounted Service School at Fort Riley, where he was designated "Master of the Sword," the first Army officer to receive the honor.

Diary of the Instructor in Swordsmanship is divided into two sections. The first section, "Courses and Methods of Instruction in Swordsmanship at the Mounted Service School," outlines the three phases of saber instruction. It details the first phase, which introduces the basics to beginners, first dismounted and then on horseback. The second section, "Diary of the Master of the Sword," covers the second phase of instruction, point fencing.

This was not Patton's first publication on the topic. The year before Patton had authored *Saber Exercise 1914*, the official Army training manual on the use of the saber. But while *Saber Exercise 1914* had been carefully staffed and edited by the War Department before its official release, Patton compiled this *Diary* at the request of his student officers. He did not intend it to replace his earlier publication, but instead augment it with additional detail and guidance on a more informal level.

As a result, some passages read more polished than others—some are detailed lessons, meticulously explained and supported by accompanying graphics and photographs; while others more closely resemble quickly jotted notes. Sprinkled throughout are Patton's personal recommendations and opinions. For example, he explains why it is important to teach Army officers the art of fencing but only provide limited instruction to enlisted soldiers—and how training in swordsmanship helped troopers develop more aggressive instincts for battle. You can almost hear his voice, much younger, but still unmistakably Patton.

Aleksandra M. Rohde
Silver Spring, Maryland
March 2016

COURSES AND METHODS OF INSTRUCTION IN SWORDSMANSHIP AT THE MOUNTED SERVICE SCHOOL

The Course in Swordsmanship is divided into three distinct phases.

The **first phase** and that which is of the most importance deals with instruction in the use of the regulation saber dismounted and mounted.

It follows the provisions of *Saber Exercise 1914*, showing in detail the method of instruction therein laid down, and also explaining additional methods of instruction which, when time and facilities permit, add greatly to the efficiency of the training.

The **second phase** of instruction is Point Fencing Dismounted.

This instruction follows the general idea and rules of Dueling Sword Fencing as practiced in Europe, but has for its object, not the making of a Fencing Room Champion but of stimulating by means of a **diverting gymnastic exercise** the instinctive use of the point. This exercise must not be confounded with foil fencing, from which it is totally different.

This instruction is only carried to a point which will enable the student here to grasp the ground ideas and master a sufficiently correct position to enable him to act as an instructor in the troop.

The exercise of Point Fencing as taught here may well be substituted during winter months in garrison for the periods usually applied to gymnasium work. And since it keeps the men interested and exercised while developing the idea of thrusting, it will produce better results than the perfunctory work on gymnasium apparatus, ever does.

The **third phase** of instruction comprises gymnastic saber fencing dismounted, using both point and edge.

The object of this is almost entirely gymnastic and in the nature of a suppling exercise.

Whatever military value it possesses, arises from the fact that it teaches the parrying of cuts and might conceivably save the life of an officer in some mêlée.

But on account of this very fact of parrying it must not be taught to the enlisted men of the troops. The brief instruction allotted to them must all be for the purpose of creating **vigorous, offensive, thrusting fighters.** And since it is the nature of men to be defensive in personal combat with arms, this exercise must never be indulged in. The saber whenever used is used tactically—not for individual defense.

The men must be impressed with the idea that the proper defense is a transfixed opponent.

————————

The following is the diary of the instructor at the Mounted Service School in teaching the **first phase**, the use of the regulation saber.

Each lesson lasts one hour.

Lesson 1.

Using light fencing saber (or wooden ordnance fencing saber if necessary) show the position of the hand on the grip with reference to the service saber. Instructor demonstrates with service saber.

Whenever conformation of hand permits the thumb in its entire length, including first joint at the wrist, must lie along the back of the grip.

Soldiers have a tendency to let the thumb cross the back of the grip diagonally.

Show position of thumb in lower half of thumb groove.

The object of first lessons is to develop the mind before the muscles. If a heavy saber is used at first the mind wanders on account of fatigued muscles. Hence use a fencing sword or simply a stick at first, later develop the muscles as per paragraph 4, *Saber Exercise 1914.*

Also in battle a man is excited and feels the weight of his sword less than in the cold blood of drill.

2

The weight is necessary in order to give required stiffness and weight to deflect an opponent's thrust.

Show the position of all the Guards. Insist that in all of these except left front guard, the blade and forearm form one straight line.

In left front guard the sword and forearm are in the same horizontal plane.

Being in any position, except one of the other four guards. Right front guard is taken at the command: Guard.

To avoid confusion when in one of the other Guards, as for example: Guard to the right, to resume guard, to the right front, give the command: Right Front Guard.

The change from one guard to the other is done in the simplest manner. When passing from the right side to the left side raise the blade sufficiently to clear the imaginary position of the horse's head. This must be insisted on so that the recruit will form the habit and not strike his horse in the head when mounted.

Lesson 2.

Repeat the first lesson.

The expression blade and forearm forming one straight line, seems to cause some confusion. Men get it in a straight line viewed from above (sword and arm in same vertical plane), but never seem to get it in the same straight line viewed from the side. They usually bend the wrist up.

Correct this by taking hold of the individual swords and placing them properly. Insist on absolutely correct positions.

Have practice in changing from one guard to another at command.

At the last part of lesson show right front and left front point. Explain the necessity for rotating the wrist in returning to guard from right front point. This rotation is necessary in returning to guard from right front point, right front lunge and charge saber, **and in no other cases**, for the following reasons.

In any of these positions the saber enters the objective with the edge of the blade up. If the swordsman while galloping past his objective, attempts to withdraw the blade without giving the prescribed rotation he bends the flat of the blade against the wound in the objective and if he is not disarmed he will break his blade. If he makes the proper rotation he brings the edge of the blade against the wound and there is no danger of bending or breaking, while the double-edge of the blade cuts its way out.

Again if he does not make the rotation, he starts to withdraw the blade with his hand upside down in a position which allows no play to the fingers and little to the wrist. The pommel acts as the end of a lever against the wrist as a point of support and the blade is wrenched from his hand or his wrist is sprained, or both.

If he rotates his hand promptly the wrist and fingers will have maximum play and the blade will be easily withdrawn.

This rotation must be absolutely insisted upon in dismounted and all subsequent work so as to form the habit and cause the movement to become second nature. For when attacking dummies mounted it must be performed in a fraction of a second and while disturbed by the restive horse.

The requirement that the left hand be kept six inches in front of the belt buckle must be rigidly enforced so that the student will learn to control the action of his left hand and not jerk his horse's mouth when mounted. Men have a tendency to hug themselves with the left arm, doing so, prevents their learning the necessary control.

Lesson 3.

Review preceding lessons. Explain Right Point, Left Point and Right Rear Point.

The reason for turning the edge of the blade up in the left point is that by so doing an increased reach of about three inches is gained.

In point to the right the hilt should travel up a little faster than the point, so that at all stages of the extension the hilt is higher than the point. The reason for this is to protect the body at all times from a rear cut or thrust by the adversary.

Give two or more points at one command. By the command: 1. **To the right**; 2. **Two times**; 3. **POINT**. Execute the indicated number of points coming accurately to the guard between each successive point.

Have points executed from some other guard. Left Point; from right front guard.

If being in Left Guard the command is: 1. **To the right**; 2. **Three times**; 3. **POINT**. The student executes right point, resumes right guard for an instant, points to the right again; resumes right guard, points to the right a third time and then returns to left guard.

No matter from what guard right front point is made, the rotation must be executed before returning to the guard where the movement started.

Practice the preceding exercises correcting faults. Insist on increased speed as proficiency increases.

Lesson 4.

Review points and guards. Cause men to execute a number of points first from proper guard, then from any guard. In order to correct positions, give command: 1. To the left; 2. And hold it; 3. POINT. When the necessary correction has been made, resume left front guard by command: GUARD.

Have several different points executed at one command for example: 1. To the right front and right; 2. POINT.

Explain points of precision.
Explain extending points into lunges.

5

Explain stretching exercises.

These exercises were devised by Sergeant Dimond, the assistant instructor, for the purpose of limbering up recruits. They are executed by the command 1. **Stretching exercises**; 2. **GUARD**. 1. **Right front**; 2. **Point**; 3. **Stretch**; 4. **GUARD**.

At the command **POINT** the indicated point is taken and held. At the command **STRETCH** the man stretches in the direction he is pointing as far as he can and keeps on trying to increase his reach until the command **GUARD** when he resumes the guard from which he started.

Practice the above, speeding up as soon as possible in everything except the stretches which are always done slowly.

Lesson 5.

Review the preceding lessons giving special practice in Points of Precision and the Lunges.

The last five minutes have lunges and points and guards done with the regulation saber.

Lesson 6.

Stretching exercises. Guards. Points. Lunges. Points of Precision.

In the points and lunges speed up and especially insist on a rapid and correct resumption of guard after each point or lunge.

Lunges at the right moment.

See that everyone understands the object of this lunge and pay particular attention to having the students make a full extension and properly and instantly resume guard.

If this detail is not watched carefully the lunge will be half hearted and the return to guard faulty.

Always insist that the instructor continue on past the student after he is touched. If this is not done the necessity for a quick return to guard will not appear.

Finish lesson by a few minutes use of the regulation saber, making points and lunges.

6

Lesson 7.

Stretching exercises. Guards. Points. Lunges. In giving these, continually insist on more speed and accuracy.

Points of precision. In these and similar exercises see that the acting instructor does not violate the principles of Figure 1, Page 13, *Saber Exercise 1914*.

Finish with regulation sabers, giving fewer rests.

Where possible have points of precision with regulation saber using a dummy and pointer as per paragraph 18, *Saber Exercise 1914*.

Lesson 8.

Guards. Points. Lunges. Points of Precision. Lunges at the right moment. Where possible have the student mounted on the wooden horse and use fencing saber against an instructor. Then regulation sabers against a dummy on wheels.

Here the necessity for the rotation in lunges, etc., to the right front will become obvious.

Harp on this until the student executes the movement properly and at once resumes guard.

The first two or three times the dummy is wheeled at him it is best to have him in the position of Charge Saber so that he will become fearless in meeting the dummy squarely with his outstretched arm. Be sure to go slowly at first so as not to arouse his apprehension.

Exercises to develop initiative.

At first see that the acting instructor makes very slight dodges and that the student comes to an accurate guard between his first and second lunge. Also see that in both lunges he makes a full extension.

If some man is particularly slow simply insist that whether or not the instructor avoids the first lunge, he lunge a second time anyway.

This exercise is very important and the more slow and stupid the recruit the more necessary is the exercise.

7

Note: The wooden horse is made low so that the instructor on foot will be as high as the man on the horse. This gives the same effect as if both were mounted.

Lesson 9.

Review preceding lessons and see that all understand thoroughly what they have had up to this point. Several reviews may be necessary to insure the above requisites. Accomplish this before proceeding further.

Lesson 10.

Reply to Attack.

Carry out exactly the letter and spirit of these exercises as laid down in *Saber Exercise 1914.*

At first the instructor uses his saber very little. Bending all his energies to causing the student to disregard it and strive to touch with the point. The attitude of mind of the student should be that of a catcher in baseball, who is bent on getting the ball regardless of the bat of the batsman. So the soldier must get his point in regardless of the sword of his opponent. And if he lunges as he has been taught he will get his point in and at the same time deflect the point or edge of his opponent. This is the point to impress on him. Hence at first the instructor makes very slow and faulty attacks insisting that the student disregard them and touch him.

Later when the instructor uses more vigor the student will see that by a proper lunge, he hits his man and covers himself. In the first lesson the instructor uses only the edge, as this is easiest for the student.

If possible have the last part of this lesson with student on wooden horse.

Review previous lessons and exercises with regulation saber, except, of course, combat.

Lesson 11.

Review exercises to develop initiative seeing that in it the first lunges are always at the right moment and fully extended.

In exercises in Reply to Attack, the instructor will begin to use the point. Lunging too soon, too late, too high or low.

The student still must disregard the instructor's blade and strive to touch. If he encounters the blade in his attempt to touch, he simply regards it as an incident; the very act of lunging; brushes it aside and he goes on to this touch.

His lunge, if properly made, will always find the opponent's blade on the outside; if it does not, the lunge is not properly made. By the outside, I mean that in lunging to the right front the opposing blade **must** be to the right of his blade. Lunging to the left front the opposing blade **must** be to the left.

The above ought to be clear, but some people don't seem to appreciate it. By having the opposing weapon **always** to the outside you deflect it in the way the motion of the horse already gives it a tendency to move. If you deflect it to the inside you oppose your strength to the momentum of twelve hundred pounds of man and horse running at twenty miles an hour. And if you deflect it at all, it is right into your own body.

The exercise of Reply to Attack is the thing for which all preceding exercises have been working up. It should be practiced extensively and not unduly hurried.

It is conducted in the sequence of (e) paragraph 25, *Saber Exercise 1914.*

Part of these exercises should be with trooper mounted on wooden horse.

Practice with regulation saber.

Lesson 12.

Guards. Points. Lunges. Charge Saber. A few lunges at the right moment. Then commence reply to attack and combine with it exercises to develop initiative.

For example, the trooper is on guard. The armed instructor approaches from his right front. He avoids the lunge, passes on by his right and makes a right rear cut. The student must return to guard and instantly lunge to the right with his hilt higher than his point; this will parry the cut and he will also get in his point. It should be demonstrated that the farther he lunges to the right the better will be his chance of avoiding the cut and of getting in his thrust.

If the instructor uses the point the student lunges as before being sure to encounter his opponent's blade, so as to force it to his rear. That is, in the direction in which it is going.

The same exercises must be carried out to the left front and left.

If he is attacked from his right rear he must again force his opponent's blade to the outside. Always he must accommodate his lunge in opposition, i.e., his parry to the direction in which his opponent's blade is moving.

It should here be pointed out that in lunging to the right rear, the farther he leans back, the smaller target he exposes and also the greater his reach.

The principal which causes the swordsman to always deflect his opponent's blade in the way it is already moving is the same as that which many line men in football sometimes use in making an opening. Instead of trying to force their opponent back, they assist his charge by pulling him forward and deflecting him to one side, using his own momentum to affect his downfall.

This exercise should also be practiced with the student mounted on the wooden horse.

In lunging on the wooden horse, care should be taken from the first that the student keeps his lower leg in place. There is a tendency to let the legs fly to the rear. Such an act on a live horse would make him run away. He would associate every lunge with a blow of the spur and be ruined as a charger.

These exercises in sequence of paragraph 25, *Saber Exercise 1914.*

Lesson 13.

Exercises of Combat.

After these exercises have been carried out as in *Saber Exercise 1914*, mount the student on the Wooden Horse and place two or more men in the places indicated for each assistant in Figure 2, *Saber Exercise 1914.* The instructor standing at the left rear can then cause them to attack in any order and at any gait. For example, he may have two attacks from the right front in quick succession, followed by one from the left front and another from the right rear. In fact anything that will keep the student awake. The men making the attacks may dodge the first lunge and make a cut or thrust in passing.

Owing to the difficulty of seeing to the rear with a mask on the instructor may, if he sees fit, give warning of an attack from the rear by calling: Rear.

In the second Combat Exercise, figure 3, "Saber Exercise 1914," after the student has been well drilled in it, the instructor will have the assistants stand still and let the student pass through and cause the last assistant in the right column to face about and attack the student from the left rear as he passes.

To see if the student remembers to incline to the left and circle to the right as he has been told to do.

Every lesson like the above should be ended with a few lunges at the right moment, because in the excitement of the combat exercises, the men are apt to lunge too short or too late and this will correct the fault. Preferably it should be on the wooden horse with a regulation saber against the rolling dummy. Insist on great exactness.

When the student has reached this stage, Right Front Guard is maintained habitually. In lunging in any other direction he simply passes through the corresponding guard in the act of lunging.

Lesson 14.

While it is hardly probable that we will encounter troops armed with the lance it is still possible, and in such a case some knowledge of how to combat it will be useful.

Take a pole about ten feet long and an inch to an inch and a quarter in diameter. Place a leather pad at one end.

The instructor grasps this a little in rear of the balance with the butt under his right arm. He walks toward the student's right front and just before reaching him he extends his arm so that the lance shaft lies along under his arm from waist to arm pit. Or he may simply hold it with the arm bent as at first described. Foreign nations use both methods usually making the lunge only when going slowly and against another lance or bayonet.

The student armed with his saber lunges at the right moment as described but he estimates this moment with reference to the point of the lance; not the body of his opponent as he would were the latter armed with a saber.

Having made his lunge he encounters the point on the outside of his saber and lets his saber slide the length of the shaft, forcing the lance to the outside and gaining his touch by keeping his point directed at the body of the lancer.

The theory of this attack rests on the fact that the saber being shorter than the lance as the two weapons slide along each other, the forte of the saber is reached before the forte of the lance, so that the saber has power to deflect the lance. In practice this is true.

In attacking to the left front the lancer rests his lance across his bridle arm and so has a stronger support for his weapon and is more deadly. Here too, a lunge at the right moment as described will deflect it.

When attacked from his left rear the lancer turns in his saddle and rests the lance in the bend of his bridle arm.

To his right rear he changes ends with his lance and has the point coming out under his arm it. This is his weakest position.

In single combat lancers make moulinets but this phase need not be dealt with, as here our men would best use the pistol.

It must always be remembered that the saber is for tactical offensive. And the idea to charge with the point must be the dominant idea in teaching its use.

MOUNTED WORK.

Lesson 1.

When using green horses, have men mount without arms and cause horses to move in straight lines, in spite of changes of position on the part of the rider. Have them pass close to each other going in opposite directions and encourage them to not swerve off.

The above should be practiced at walk, trot and gallop, increasing the gait as the horses go well at the one below. A few dummies should be in the vicinity, but make no effort to force the horses up to them; simply disregard their presence and the horses will never be frightened.

Horses should be well worked out by ordinary work before beginning the above lesson. And in all subsequent lessons it will be assumed that the horses are fairly well tried and worked down. This makes them less restive and is also the condition which would exist in war.

Lesson 2.

Men without arms take the various guard positions at the halt, then the motions of all the points. Then slowly extend into the lunges.

Repeat this at the walk, at the same time seeing that the horses do not swerve from a straight line. Make the changes of position slight at first and as the horse goes straight, increase them to the normal lunges, points and guards. Combine this with exercises in passing close to each other in opposite directions.

Repeat the above at the canter.

Lunges or other sword movements should never be made at the trot. As the horses go, quietly practice the lunges with more vigor, but be careful to see that the legs stay in place; if they fly back they will cause the horse to bolt.

Place some quiet horses two yards from the track on either hand and have other horses pass between them and the wall of the riding hall or other inclosure.

Lesson 3.

Have the men armed with wooden sabers. Let them ride the horses about at the walk carrying these sabers and by slowly moving them about, accustom the horses to them. Most men seem to take delight in holding the saber close to the horse's eyes or ears when first using them on him. This naturally scares him. Do not allow it.

By carrying the saber simply as an incident to the ride, he will soon accustom the horse to it.

At the halt go through the guards, points, and lunges, slowly at first; then with more snap as the horses stand quietly.

Using the swords go through the same exercises as in the previous lessons.

Change the position of the dummies daily, so that the horses will get used to them as such, and not attribute them to some fixed locality.

Lesson 4.

Repeat the previous lessons, insisting that the movements with the saber are made accurately and with speed and vigor. Pay special attention to the legs staying in place.

Place the troopers in column on the track of a riding hall or some marked off piece of ground and have them come down the length of it by twos, executing points and lunges at will and seeing that the horses move on a straight line. Do this at walk and canter.

Repeat having them execute the movements at command. Have them hold Charge Saber for increasingly long distances.

Insist on correct movements and that they do not pull the horses mouths in making various lunges.

Be sure that in executing right rear lunge they hold the pommel in the left hand so as not to hurt the horse's mouth.

Lesson 5.

Men armed with regulation saber. Go through guards, etc., at the halt to see if any horses mind the flash. Then take the track, execute points, lunges and charge saber at command while moving down length of hall by threes or fours. At walk and canter.

Lead the column of troopers among the dummies, passing close to them on each side. When the horses go quietly, let the sabers strike the dummies and their supports.

At the walk let the men attack the dummies with right front point and charge saber at will. Be very easy on horses that show fear. If necessary place or hold a can of oats at the base of the support and let the nervous horses eat some. Also let them follow closely behind quiet horses.

Lesson 6.

Go through guards, points, lunges at halt; then while moving by fours or threes at walk and canter. See that horses go in a straight line.

Place four dummies in line, about ten yards apart. Have the men move and attack these with Charge Saber at the walk, taking the charge position at least twenty yards from them.

Repeat this at a canter.

For this exercise it is best to have the dummies on the drill ground with plenty of room. Have the directions of the attack away from the stable and the other horses, so that the horses will have the least incentive to bolt. See that the men assume guard at once and do not pull up their horses too quickly, but turn them alternately to right and left after they are well past the dummies. This will prevent the tendency of the horses always to turn one way.

It is very important that in the first lessons at the gallop only the position of charge be used as it makes the men bold in reaching out well to the front and not flinching. If they use points or lunges at the right moment at first, they will flinch and through fear, lunge too late.

This lesson should be repeated until the men go boldly and execute the charge with precision and are able to hold the charge for fifty yards.

They may be sent to the attack either by fours or singly. The horses should be kept at the canter.

Lesson 7.

Execute Guards, Points, Lunges and Charge Saber at the halt and by command at the gallop.

Place a second row of dummies fifteen yards beyond first row. Have the men attack the first row with lunge at the right moment to the right front and left front; instantly resume guard and canter past the second row without attacking.

Pay particular attention to their lunging in time and not too late; and to the prompt resumption of Guard. In attacking to the left front, it is best to have them assume left front guard twenty yards or so before they make the lunge.

Next have them attack the first row at the charge, then resume the guard and attack the second row with lunge to the right front or left front at the right moment.

Here the necessity for quickly assuming Guard after the first dummy is passed will become evident. When they are to attack the second dummy to the left front it is best to have it about three yards to the left of the line of attack and the first dummy: so that in this early exercise they will have no necessity to guide the horse, who, buy going in a straight line will naturally pass the second dummy to his left.

If the condition of the horse justifies it, the dummy should be attacked at the full gallop—the charging gait; and then slow up to the maneuvering gallop to attack the second.

Lesson 8.

When the men do well at the preceding exercise, more dummies should be added and exercises similar to figures 4, 5, and 6, *Saber Exercise 1914* should be practiced. The distance between dummies should be decreased to ten yards.

These exercises may be repeated after drill, whenever practicable, care always being taken that the men get down well in the charge and have the head protected by the guard. That in the lunges they do not lunge too late and make a full and proper extension.

Note: By "get down well" is meant that in the charge and in lunging to the right front or left front the men get down so low that their chest touches the upper part of the left forearm while the under part of that arm rests on the mane.

Lesson 9.

Exercises of Pursuit. (g) paragraph 43, "Saber Exercise 1914," should be practiced occasionally as a means of relieving the monotony and to stimulate horsemanship.

Individual combat exercises should be prepared for as follows, and in any case be very sparingly indulged in as there is some risk of falls and at best they do not simulate very exactly real fights.

Have two men armed with fencing sabers and masks and jackets approach each other at the walk. When they are in the act of passing as close as possible, halt them; have them extend the swords above their heads and strike them together, at the same time soothing their horses by voice and stroking. Do this, passing on each side. When the horses go quietly, do it without halting. Then let them take right front point and left front point, striking the swords together as they pass but without trying to touch. Do the same thing, lunging to the right front and left front.

Next have them take concentric circles on opposite hands at the canter, coming as near together as they can, while passing. Have them pass on either side at command. When the horses go quietly have them execute points and lunges as they pass, striking their swords together but not attempting to touch. When all goes well, give the command: **Attack.** They continue at the same gait on the circle and the next time they pass, lunge at the right moment and strive to touch.

In order to quiet the horses it is well to let them pass a couple of times before again giving the command: Attack.

In order to show in a forceful manner the advantages of the lunge, properly made, over the edge, direct one of them to make a head, or other cut, the next time you give Attack.

If the above is carefully carried out the men and horses are ready for individual combat and combat by fours as per *Saber Exercise 1914.*

To avoid hurting the horses' eyes, the wooden fencing sabers used for this work should have a leather pad on the end. And the metal fencing saber a ball of tar tape the size of an egg on its end.

Additional Exercises.

The Saber Chute. Build a chute five feet wide and two hundred feet long, with top rail three feet high. On either side at intervals of thirty feet, place posts holding dummy swords made of a pole with a leather pad on the end, fixed to represent swords in cutting and thrusting positions. Behind each place a dummy. The trooper on a quiet horse gallops through, lunging at the right moment against each dummy and in so doing deflecting the sword and sticking the dummy. The idea is to show how the lunge both parries and attacks at the same time. The dummy swords should not be too strong or too firmly attached to their supports so that if one should hit a man, it will break and not hurt him.

Without the dummy swords this chute may also be used for teaching the simple charge as the horse has to run straight. Also by placing a dummy a little way from the railing, it makes a man reach further in lunging to the right or left.

The device with three dummies on the spokes of a horizontal wheel has for its object the development of decision and accuracy and strengthening the wrist.

The trooper gallops around the machine on a circle fifteen yards radius. He is armed with a wooden sword. At the command: **Attack,** he turns his horse on his haunches towards the center and attacks with a lunge at the right moment, the dummy nearest him. If possible he should hit hard enough for the wheel to revolve once. After he has hit it, he goes on and takes the circle again on the same hand. A platoon may be placed on the circle and the men made to attack at command. Being on the circle they are under better control.

This diary is not intended to supplant the *Saber Exercise 1914*, but simply as a system of applying the teaching therein laid down and of bringing into notice special points which experience has shown required emphasizing.

Whenever teaching men the use of the saber the *Saber Exercise 1914* should be constantly consulted and exactly followed.

GEORGE S. PATTON, JR.,
*2nd Lieut. 15th Cavalry,
Instructor in Fencing, M. S. S.*
March 20, 1915.

19

Wooden Horse and Rolling Dummy

Side Elevation—Wooden Horse

Manner of Affixing Lance at Saber Chute

Saber Chute

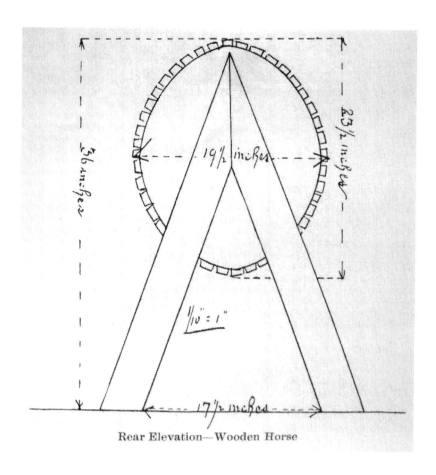

Rear Elevation—Wooden Horse

The Device with Three Dummies.

DIARY OF THE MASTER OF THE SWORD
Second Phase: Point Fencing

In presenting the follow extracts from his diary the instructor desires to disavow any pretense to the writing of a work on fencing or to the expounding of anything original.

Experienced fencers reading it will find many crudities and will be shocked at the small attention paid to accuracy. They are asked to remember, however, that it is neither the desire nor the object of the course here to teach fencing for its own sake or to make individual champions.

What we do is to use fencing as an adjunct to teaching the use of the point when fighting mounted with the regulation saber.

With this end in view, we try to teach the students here a few parries and attacks and approximately correct position, so that they may pass this instruction on to the men of their troops thus getting them interested and fairly proficient in the game of attacking each other with the point and by this means combatting in them their harmful, natural instinct to cut.

Again it must be remembered by academic instructors, that, in the Army, it is necessary to instruct many men at once, hence the speedy recourse to combat. Also, the time is very limited and the sooner the psychology of thrusting can be inculcated by actual bouts the better.

This course follows as nearly as may be the course and methods of M. L'Adjutant *Clery*, Senior Maitre d'Armes at the Cavalry School, at Saumur, France, as used by him on the non-commissioned officers who come there each summer for instruction as *escadron* assistant instructors.

The rules used here and recommended to be followed are similar to those of the Amateur Fencer's League of America governing the use of the duelling sword.

Touches: A touch on any part of the opponent's body, limbs, mask, hands or feet is valid. A touch must be such that were the sword sharp, it would draw blood. Slaps or scratches are not touches. If both attack at nearly the same time the one whose touch first lands gets the decision. If no difference in time is apparent, the one whose touch is the higher line gets the decision. Except in the case of such a touch with no difference in time, if one man is touched on his sword arm while touching his adversary on the body, the man making the arm touch would get the decision. If both touch at the same time and there is no difference in line, each is counted touched.

There is no rule requiring an attack to be parried; a Stop Thrust may always be tried.

Bouts: Usually for the one first getting three touches. The combatants change ends on the mat after each touch.

If a man steps off the side or end of the mat, he is counted as touched (mats used here are 36 feet long and 3 feet wide). Mats are useful but not necessary.

In any case, when a touch would terminate a bout, all double touches should be counted **no touch**, irrespective of difference of line; and in this case it is essential that a very distinct difference in time should be insisted on. Enforcement of this convention will do away with much bad feeling and many arguments.

A touch after disarming is not valid. A touch made in the art of disarming is valid.

Judges: For an important bout there should be four judges and a president or director.

Conduct of Bouts: The president causes the contestants to come on guard, crossing their swords over his at the center of the mat. He then commands: **Retreat**. Each retires one step so that there is a clear space between the points of their swords. He then commands: **Fence**, upon which they attack each other.

The four judges are arranged as per Figure No. 1. Judge number 1 watches B's right side, Judge number 3 his left side, Judge number 2 watches A's left side and Judge number 4 his right side. They also watch in a general way for all touches. The president watches everything, but especially the time in a double touch.

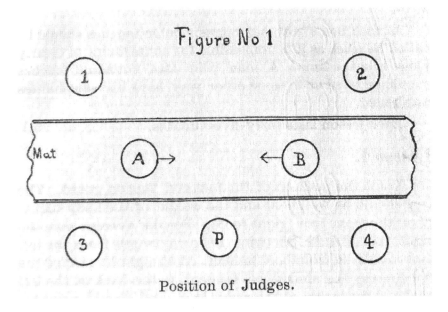

Position of Judges.

If any one of the judges sees what appears to him to be a touch, he calls **Halt**, upon which the contestants stand fast and lower their swords. The president asks the judge calling halt where he saw the touch. He then asks each of the other judges if they saw a touch there or anywhere else. The president awards the touch by the vote of the majority, if there is a tie the president votes to break it. The president's opinion is final on questions of time. If after a halt has been called it is decided that there was no touch, the bout re-commences at the part of the mat where the halt was called by the same procedure as at first. If a touch was awarded, the contestants, return to the middle, change ends and commence as before. Nos. 1 and 3 now watch A; Nos. 2 and 4 watch B. In the case of a double touch being called **No touch** because it would have ended the bout, the contestants continue to combat where they were without changing ends or returning to the center.

(Cut No. 1)   Guard

When men fence without judges they should call **Touch** if they feel anything at all, and the man making it should, **as a point of honor**, disclaim it if he thinks that what his opponent called a touch was a scratch or a flat.

In such bouts without judges, double touches should be called **No touch** as it is impossible for contestants to clearly judge relative time. A man who does not admit touches should be tried or in some other way have his sensibilities awakened.

Each lesson lasts forty-five minutes.

Lesson 1.

Teach the position of the feet and legs on guard. The legs should be well bent and the weight of the body slightly on the front foot (right foot). For the average man the right foot should be twice its own length from the left foot measured from heel to heel. A straight line called the **directing line** should be tangent to the back of the left heel and the inside of the right heel, and should point toward the adversary. The right foot should be well turned out and the left should be perpendicular to the directing line. Unless the right foot is watched carefully the men will turn it in, to the detriment of their position and balance, and the length of their lunge. Moreover this faulty position also makes them likely to turn their ankles.

The right thigh bone and shin bone must be in a plane perpendicular to the ground though the tendency is to incline the lower leg to the left.

The back must not be swayed but must be convex, with the buttocks well under. The center of gravity is over the directing line.

The position of the right arm should be such that the forearm is covered by the bell (guard) of the sword. The point should be slightly lower than the hilt, the pommel against the wrist. The thumb should be up and the arm a little more than half extended. (See Cut No. 1)

31

The guard described above is called by fencers the **median guard**. The line of the shoulders should be as nearly as possible parallel to the directing line. The left hand rests on the left hip bone with the left elbow well to the rear. This position of the left hand is not so good as the academic position with it raised, but the experience of good teachers shows that with the trooper it is impossible to get the proper position with the left hand raised and as an improper one is awkward the position on the hip is recommended as being the best substitute.

After the men have been placed properly in this position let them relax and then try to resume it at will. Continue this until they get the correct position.

Lesson 2.

Review Lesson 1. Show mechanism of advance and retreat. In both these movements the feet should stay close to the ground. In the advance, the right foot moves first, in the retreat, the left. This should be practiced until the men execute it smoothly.

Explain the lunge. The impetus for this should be given by a violent extension of the left leg, the left foot remaining in place with the entire sole on the ground. The right foot should be raised the least possible and should slip to the front without noise; there must be no pounding of the foot on the ground.

The lunge should not be too long and should end with the right knee in advance of the right ankle, not with the ankle far in advance of the knee. The former position gives a greater reach and, above all, insures a quick recovery. The recovery is made by a violent extension of the right leg, the body still remaining inclined to the front, rather than by a change of balance caused by throwing the body to the rear. This is because the action of the muscles in recovery gives more speed and insures proper position when the guard is first regained.

After the students thoroughly understand the lunge, have them execute it by the command: 1. **Extend Arm**; 2. **Lunge**; 3. **GUARD**. In resuming the guard the sword arm must be left fully extended with the hand about the height of the chin, the point menacing the arm or shoulder of the adversary until guard is reached and balance assured; then the normal position of the arm on guard is resumed.

The object of this is to threaten the opponent with your point and keep him at a distance while you are recovering from the crucial situation resulting from an unsuccessful attack. You, so to speak, **vanish behind your point**.

When a man is expert it is perfectly proper for him to parry as he recovers, preparatory to a second lunge or to a simple riposte without lunging. Few soldiers will attain this proficiency, and in consequence, the above method with the arm extended is far safer for them.

The following is a good exercise. 1. **Extend Arm**; 2. **Advance**; 3. **Retreat**; 4. **Lunge**; 5. **GUARD**. The advance or retreat may be repeated two or more times or one or the other may be omitted; it is useful, however, to frequently give Lunge, immediately following Retreat, so as to make the men drive forward from their left leg and also to practice them in rapid changes from defense to offense. The above exercise is on exactly the same theory as that by which a horse is collected by moving him forward, halting, backing and moving forward again.

Lesson 3.

Review previous lessons paying particular attention to accurate position and rapid execution of the movements. Pair off the men and place one to act as a target at such a distance that the other can reach him easily with his point in the lunge, then give **Retreat**, **Advance**, **Extend Arm**, and **Lunge**, having the movements executed inversely by the man acting as target. For example when you say: 1. **Extend Arm**; 2. **Advance**; 3. **Lunge**; 4. **GUARD**: the man with the sword advances while the target retreats the same amount and so on.

When the sword touches the target the blade should bend so that the arc it forms is convex upward, not the reverse. The sword hand should raise slightly just as the touch is made and the grip should be partially relaxed. There is a tendency to let the hand fall as the touch is made; this is due, I believe, to an instinctive attempt to support the weight of the body by the blade: it is conducive to lack of balance and is a sign of it. Also the normal riposte is in the high line and by raising the hand the attacker in resuming his guard covers his sword arm and part of his body whereas by lowering the hand he exposes himself.

This rule is, of course, very elastic. For example, in a lunge in opposition from the high line the hand must be lowered or again in the case of an Underbind and in other special cases too numerous to be specified here.

After the men execute the preceding exercise correctly, omit the command **Extend Arm**; simply give **LUNGE**, but insist that the arm be fully extended before the foot moves. This must be very carefully watched, as the natural tendency is to advance the foot and then poke with the sword. If this habit is ever formed it is almost impossible to break it.

At this period there must be a clear, though brief, instant between the extension of the arm and the movement of the foot in the lunge. In the recovery insist that the arm stays extended until the balance on guard is assured.

Too much emphasis cannot be laid on the above requirements. I shall recapitulate these points the better to vivify them. In the lunge the body is shot forward by the violent extension of the muscles of the left thigh, the right foot is barely raised from the ground, the right heel landing first. The guard is resumed by a similar extension of the muscles of the right thigh.

The average man does not do either of these things; he lets the body fall to the front by balance and in resuming guard he throws his weight to the rear and arrives on guard by the action of gravity, his right toe pointing down. It is quite obvious that movements by gravity are bound to be slower than those by muscular force. The sprinter does not fall off his **marks**; he kicks himself off with his hind leg as should the fencer in the lunge.

An instructor can usually tell when a man is resuming guard properly by noticing that when he does so his right toe is up, not down, as he goes to the rear. Moreover the shift of the weight in a lunge by balance is always visible to the adversary. Prior to a lunge by balance the weight must be moved to the front, hence the right leg becomes overloaded and it is harder to shoot it forward. In the lunge the right foot is not slammed down; it is slid to the front barely clearing the ground. The heel on landing is still tangent to the directing line with the toe slightly turned out.

At first the lunge should be short so at its completion the right knee is over the right toe, never so that the toe is far in advance of the knee. In the first case the forward movement is only checked by the elasticity of the muscles; in the second case the lunger is brought up short, bumping, so to speak into the stiff column of the leg bones. Also in the correct lunge the thigh muscles are stretched more, giving in consequence a greater opportunity for contraction and thus shooting the man back to guard more promptly. The lunge should never be held; the guard must always be resumed with maximum speed. In extending the arm before a lunge the movement must be confined to the arm and shoulder; the body and legs must not move.

Lesson 4.

Review all the preceding lessons paying particular attention to correct position and to accuracy in all movements. Insist that the recovery from the lunge be as rapid as possible. It is a bad practice to cause a student to hold his lunge. This is sometimes necessary to make corrections but should always be followed by several lunges with instantaneous recoveries.

I will at this point describe the four simple parries, so that they may hereafter be referred to without further description. The four simple parries are: **Right High Direct, Left High Direct, Right Low Direct,** and **Left Low Direct.**

In a Right High Direct the point is raised so that the blade makes an angle of about 30 degrees above horizontal, the right hand with the arm almost extended is carried to the right sufficiently to deflect the opponent's blade from the point of attack. In this movement the point should remain fixed in space, the guard moving to the right thus always keeping the point in line for the opponent's breast. This is facilitated by retaining the hand to the right so that the nails are up and at the same time bending the wrist slightly to the left. Most beginners will move the hand with a stiff wrist and no rotation consequently carrying the point far out of line to the right. Also they will move the hand farther than is necessary thus losing much time in the recovery and facilitating a disengagement on the part of the opponent.

Right Low Direct is made in exactly the same way except that the point is lower so that the blade makes an angle of about 30 degrees below the horizontal.

In Left Low Direct the point is raised as in Right High Direct, the hand is carried to the left sufficiently to deflect the enemy's point from the threatened spot. In this case the point is kept in line by rotating the hand to the left so that the nails are down and the wrist bent slightly to the right.

Left Low Direct is made in the same way except the blade makes an angle of 30 degrees below the horizontal.

In all Direct Parries the tendency to draw the hand back towards the body must be combatted. It is quite obvious that the further away from the body the parry is made the less will the hand have to move to cause an equal deflection of the opponent's blade. The arm, in parrying, is not fully extended because this would give the opponent too great a chance to overbind. Having defined the Direct Parries, I shall proceed with the lesson.

An instructor takes each student and causes him to come on guard facing him, that is, to engage. In the engagement there is no crossing of blades or **feeling**. The instructor and student face each other on guard at such a distance that their respective points reach to within an inch or so of the other's guard. Each has his blade parallel and to the right of that of his opponent. The point of each should threaten the inside edge of the opponent's bell (guard). This is called **keeping the point in line in the guard**. This keeping of the point in line must be insisted on as there is a tendency to have the point too high or too low and too far to the right. (See Cuts No. 2 & 3).

(Cut No. 2) Engagement

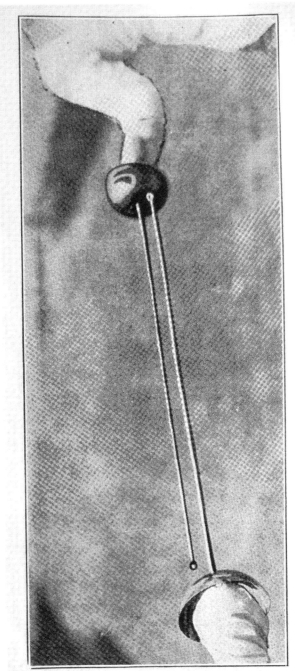

(Cut No. 3)   Engagement

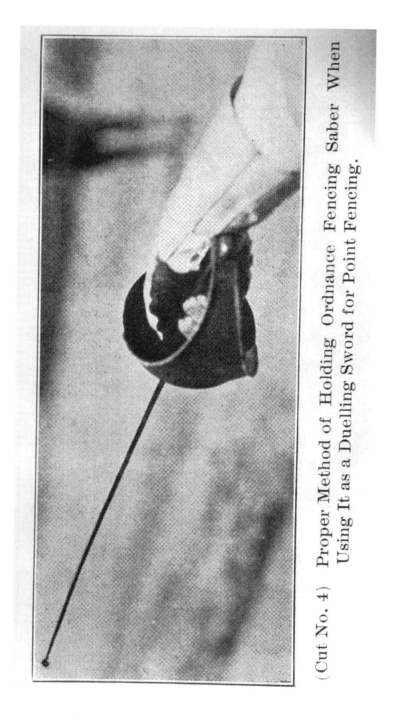

(Cut No. 4) Proper Method of Holding Ordnance Fencing Saber When Using It as a Duelling Sword for Point Fencing.

Having gotten a proper engagement the instructor shows the student Attack No. 1. This is a One-Two. The student feints direct at the instructor's chest by extending the arm and shoulder as much as he can without moving the legs. The instructor parries Left High Direct; as soon as his blade starts to move in the parry, the student should disengage below and lunge for his chest on the outside of his sword. The disengagement must be made with the fingers and wrist, the arm remains fully extended. The lunge must not be made until the blade is straightened out in the new direction.

In order to make the student use a small disengagement it is well to advise him to have in his mind to lunge for the position occupied by the guard of the instructor's sword before it started to move in the first parry. In order to determine the accuracy of the student the instructor should not, at first, parry the lunge, but should insist on an accurate recovery.

Note: On account of the bruises caused by being lunged at many times, the instructor should wear a pad made by the saddler out of a double thickness of old blanket faced with leather.

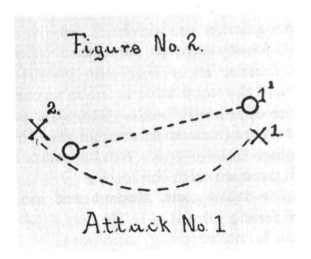

Figure No. 2.

Attack No. 1

Note: The diagrammatic scheme used here to represent various attacks is to be translated as follows:

The (O) indicates the projection, on a vertical plane midway between contestants, the position of the sword of the man on the defense. The (X) the projected position on the same plane, of the sword of the attacker. You are supposed to look at the plane from the position of the attacker. The lines are the projected movements of the two swords. The Nos. 1, 2 and 3, indicate successive feints by the attacker. The Nos. 1', 2', 3', the corresponding parries of the defender. The final parry in each case is omitted.

High Direct Parries are used at first as they are easiest for the student.

The above attack should be executed slowly and accurately with each student, and they should be impressed from first, with the idea that a feint must be such as to force the opponent to parry. That this is the one and only object or excuse for a feint, and that if, at any time, a feint is not parried; they must instantly convert it into an attack, by a lunge. This idea may be brought home to them from the beginning by the instructor occasionally failing to parry.

To repeat. A feint is a threat with the point, which leaves the opponent no alternative except to parry, retreat or be touched by your next movement: the lunge. Note: Throughout this diary all movements of the sword are described in English. French terms are, perhaps, more accurate, certainly more academic, but to the American soldier they are confusing.

Lesson 5.

Review the exercises of Advance, Retreat, Lunge, Guard, etc., trying always to get correct movements and to overcome natural awkwardness.

Have each man attack the instructor with Attack No. 1 taught in Lesson 4. Give Attack No. 2, a One-Two, in which the student disengages under the blade and feints at the shoulder on the right side. The instructor parries Right High, the student disengaging below the second time and lunging at the chest.

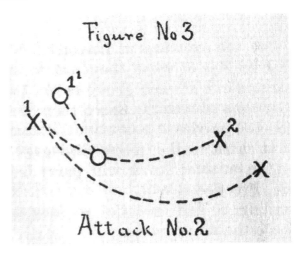

In making the first feint the student should carry his point under that of the instructor by moving the blade to his (the student's) left by his wrist and extending his arm and shoulder at the same time in the feint. As soon as the instructor starts the parry the student, by a movement of the wrist and fingers, again disengages below and as soon as the sword is straightened out for the chest, lunges. The recovery is as before, with a straight arm and high guard.

Next show them the Right and Left High Direct Parries which they have just seen the instructor execute. When they get these fairly well, which they will very readily, repeat

43

attacks Nos. 1 and 2, this time with the student on the defense, the instructor making the attacks.

In this exercise try to make them keep the bodies still and not draw in the hand, but if anything extend it as they parry. Try to keep them from getting their points too high or moving them too far out of line in the parries. At this point they are not up to keeping the point in line in the parry by bending the wrist as described, but the necessity for this should be pointed out to them.

Lesson 6.

Have each student lunge directly at the instructor without a feint. The instructor should parry and riposte at the arm or shoulder as the student recovers with a straight arm. In this way faults in their position in recovering will become evident to them and they will see that if they recover properly, they will not be touched.

Note: A riposte is a counter thrust given by a defender after a successful parry. It may be executed with or without a lunge as occasions offer, preferably however without a lunge.

Now review the exercises of Lesson 5. When all seem to get at least an idea of what they are to do, pair them off and designate one of each group as No. 1 and the other as No. 2. Give the command: **Guard**, then have them execute attacks and parries at command. Example: "No. 1. Feint direct at chest, on the parry disengage and lunge at the chest on the outside; No. 2 will parry Left and Right High Direct. Practice at will.

The wording is non-essential so long as you get the men to execute the movements.

Keep insisting that:
In the case of the defender:
The parries are no larger than necessary,
The point stays in line,
The hand is not drawn back in the parry,
The body does not move, except to avoid the touch.

In the case of the attacker:

That when the feint is once made the arm remains straight and extended,

The disengagements are small and made with the wrist,

The arm is kept straight, with a high guard in the recovery.

Hard work by the instructor at this point will be repaid later.

Lesson 7.

Review lesson 6 in toto, then show attacks Nos. 3 and 4. Attack No. 3 is just like No. 1, except that the first feint and the lunge are both directed below the line of the hand and the parries are Left and Right Low Direct, with the disengagement between the feint and parry over the sword.

Attack No. 4 is just like Attack No. 2, except that the first feint is for the outside of the elbow, and the parries are Right and Left Low Direct, with the disengagement from the feint to the lunge, over the sword. Have the men make these two attacks by command, in the same way in which they made the others.

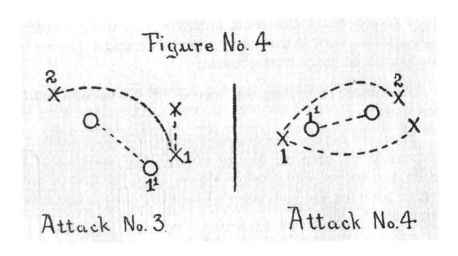

Figure No. 4

Attack No. 3   Attack No. 4

At the last part of the lesson the instructor should lunge direct at each student, causing him to parry Left or Right Low Direct and riposte at the instructor's arm or shoulder. By faulty and slow movements the instructor should give him an opportunity to touch in his riposte.

Impress the men with the fact that the riposte is very deadly and should be tried whenever possible. Besides the actual value of the riposte as a means of getting touches, the idea of trying to use it is of great assistance in making the men get and keep the point in line in the parry.

Lesson 8.

Review Lesson 7 rapidly, and then let them attack each other at will for a few moments under close supervision, one pair at a time. Be very strict with the men and see that they admit all touches and in general conduct themselves in a sportsmanlike manner. As soon as any man gets wild in his parries or fails to admit touches, stop him and give him some more exercises by command. This will have a good effect on the others as they will prefer fencing to the exercises. In the fencing be sure that the men use only the attacks taught. Beginners have a great tendency to try and invent new and ridiculous attacks, instead of perfecting themselves in what they have been taught.

At the close of the lesson teach Attack No. 5, which is a One-Two-Three. Feint (one) direct at the breast, the instructor parries Left High Direct, deceive his parry and feint (two) at the breast on the outside by disengaging below as in attack No. 1. The instructor parries Right High Direct; hold the feint until you feel the pressure of instructor's sword in the parry, then disengage (three) below again and lunge at the breast.

The object of feeling the sword in the second feint is twofold:

First—It makes the attacker acquire better control of his sword by causing him to change the cadence of his feints, the second one must be slower than the first in order to give time for the instructor's blade to get over and establish contact.

Second—Having felt the blade strongly in the Right High Direct Parry, the student suddenly removes his blade by disengaging below, and the blade of the instructor having lost its support, has a tendency to fly still further to the right, thus giving a better opening for the lunge.

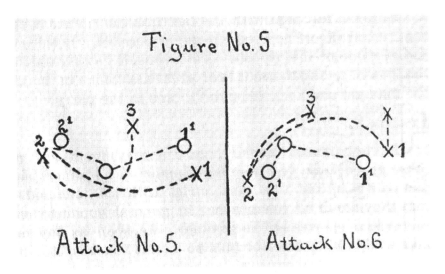

Figure No. 5

Attack No. 5.   Attack No. 6

Lesson 9.

Have the men go through with the instructor, the five attacks they have been taught, then let them fence at will. Insist that they recover properly and riposte whenever possible.

At the close of the lesson show them Attack No. 6, which is just like Attack No. 5, except that in this case the feint is a little lower and the instructor parries Left Low Direct. The student disengages above, feinting for the body on the outside. The instructor parries Right Low Direct. The student feels his blade, disengages above, and lunges for the body.

Lesson 10.

Have the men review with the instructor the six attacks and four parries they have been taught.

Show the Counter Parry Up (circular parry to the right). When the instructor makes either a feint or lunge for the body, the student, by a movement of the fingers, causes the point of his sword to describe a half circle from his right to his left, the horns of the half circle, thus formed point up. This half circle picks up the instructor's weapon from below and places it above and on the outside of the student's blade. Now by carrying the hand up and to the right, with the point slightly higher than the guard and the finger nails up, and at the same time bending the wrist to the left, the blade of the instructor is deflected to the student's right, while the student's point still stays in line. In other words, having picked up the blade of the instructor with the semi-circular movement, the student carries it to his right, with a Right High Direct Parry.

The two chief errors made by beginners with this parry is; that they either make a complete circle, thus releasing the opponents blade under their own hand and giving him an excellent chance for a thrust, or they make the half circle properly, but in carrying the hand to the right, do not bend the wrist to the left so that their point is high and to the right and consequently much out of line. Thus they lose possession of the opponent's blade, as in the case where they make a complete circle.

Counter Parry Down (circular parry to the left), is made in the same way, by describing a half circle from the student's right to his left, but in this case the horns of a half circle described point downward. When the adversary's blade has been picked up by the half circle, the hand is carried to the right, finger nails down, the point slightly lower than the guard and the wrist bent to the left. In this case the instructor's blade is below and outside that of the student. In other words, having picked up the blade by the half circle, execute a Left Low Direct Parry.

48

In this parry there is less likelihood of erring by making a complete circle, but much more danger of carrying the point too low and out of line to the right, particularly when this parry is used against a feint. This fault gives the opponent a chance to disengage above and lunge at the now unprotected body. There are other Counter Parries made from other guards but on the same method.

Either of these parries will pick up almost any direct attack or feint, but Counter Parry Up is in my experience the more useful of the two.

The only objection I see to the use of these parries is that if too slowly executed or too frequently used, they can be easily deceived.

Now cause the student to attack with any of the One-Twos so far taught, and warn him that the instructor will use any of the six parries, in irregular sequence, so that he must make his disengagement according to the parry.

This exercise is excellent to develop versatility in the student, and cause him to take an opening instantly on seeing it. Because he cannot predetermine his disengagement he must learn to seize the opening instantly and correctly, as soon as he has drawn a parry. This versatility and quickness constitutes the art of fence, after the mechanism of the movement has been learned.

While the instructor is going through the above with individual students, let the others fence at will, or have them alternately attack and defend.

Lesson 11.

The exercises contained in the preceding ten lessons, form an excellent ground work for troop fencing and should be repeated daily, with as many members of the class as time allows, those not being specially taught should be required to fence at will or practice alternate attack and defense. In order to correct the position of the arm, devote the last five minutes daily to fencing in which only the right arm is attacked. By this means, faults will be rapidly brought home to the man committing them.

The lessons which follow, should only be taken when the preceding exercises are well mastered, and in fact, it will probably be found, that only a selected number of men in a troop, will ever progress sufficiently to warrant their being carried further.

When the men fence, using the methods of the first ten lessons, they will have accomplished the psychological object of this course in fencing, namely: the stimulation in the men of a desire to thrust and thrust accurately in battle.

Lesson 12.

Show the Overbind.

This attack may be used to advantage, against an opponent who holds a feint in the high line too long, or who fences with too straight an arm. The opponent's arm being straight; disengage over his blade, pressing down on his feeble with the forte of your own blade, but make this disengagement with the elbow still bent a little. When you have forced his blade down a trifle, extend your arm vigorously, lunging for his belly; raising your guard at the same time, to a point opposite your shoulder and at the level of your eyes. This movement forces his blade up and to the right. Should you miss the touch, your opponent must disengage over your hand before he can riposte. Hence: by carrying it high as directed, you give yourself more time to recover before he can make the disengagement.

The Overbind, above described, must come as a surprise to be successful and is most dangerous, when the man on whom it is tried has his elbow so extended as to be locked straight.

The defense against this attack is to stiffen your arm so as to force the blade of the man trying the bind, to your right. Riposte at once in the low line for the belly.

The Underbind is used against a man who carries his hand on guard, too low and too far to his left, with a bent elbow.

Disengage below and pass your blade over that of your adversary from his outside, lunge for the center of his body, forcing your guard down as you do so. This places his sword below and slightly to the left of yours. To riposte he must disengage below your hand. By carrying your guard low, you gain time to recover should you have missed the touch.

The best defense against this attack is to stiffen the arm and extend it, raising the hand to the right thus forcing the blade of the man trying the Underbind, to your outside.

In order to make subsequent remarks more clear a rough definition of lines in fencing is entered here.

In theory, the position occupied by the hand in the normal guard, should be such that it is equally distant from all points of the body liable to be attacked. And that it holds the point of your sword, so that it is equally distant from all points which you wish to menace on the body of your opponent.

When the hand fulfills these requirements all points of your body above it are said to be in the High Line; all points below it in the Low Line. All points to the right OUTSIDE; all points to the left INSIDE. Thus all points of your body and that of your assailant may be separated into four segments; Outside High, Inside High, Outside Low, Inside Low.

For example: In attack No. 1, you feint at the Inside High Line of your opponent and lunge at the Outside High.

The above four segments, have been subdivided in many and various ways, by different treatises on fencing and named either according to their position, or to the manner in which they were attacked. But beyond the rough outline here given, the subject has no value, in the simple instruction to be given the soldier.

Lesson 13.

Beats.

Attacks made by the use of beats are very numerous but as they have a tendency, especially with poorly trained fencers to engender the use of large gross movements, the expedience of devoting much time to them with the men of a troop is doubtful.

Speaking in general, to execute an attack by a beat, you strike the feeble of your opponent's blade with the forte of your own and instantly lunge in the line which you have thus opened, by forcing his sword out of its normal position. Or you may beat and when he hurriedly brings his blade back to cover the line you have opened, you may disengage and lunge in some other line which in his ill calculated recovery he has left open.

For example: if you beat his blade to his outside as if to clear away to lunge in the inside, he will probably hasten to cover his inside and by overdoing it expose his outside or at least the outside of his forearm, to your disengagement and lunge.

The man making the beat must have absolute control of his blade, so that it will stop the instant after it has struck the blade of his opponent and be ready at once to proceed with the lunge, or a disengagement and lunge, as occasion offers.

The best defense against beats is a flexible and elastic wrist, which instantly brings the sword back to its original position. Or one may deceive a beat and instantly lunge in the opening which the opponent will probably leave, because his blade, not finding the looked for resistance, will go farther than he expected. A lunge in opposition is nearly allied to a beat and a bind. In fact it is a sort of hybrid of them. It is an attack made by forcing an opening by pushing the opponent's blade out of the way as you make a lunge. For example: if being in the normal engage, lunges to the Inside Low while carrying his hand forcibly high and to his left, he is executing a lunge in opposition, of the simplest sort. His adversary may escape by stiffening his arm and carrying it to his left, in a Left Low Direct Parry or by making a Counter Parry Up or Down, or by retreating.

Lesson 14.

Stops, times and counter thrusts.

A Stop Thrust is a thrust delivered against an exposed part of your opponent, usually arm or shoulder, who is making a vigorous attack or rush. As the thrust is delivered, the right foot is brought up near the left and guard raised. The whole figure of the man, executing this Stop Thrust from his right toe to the point of his sword assumes the general form of a half circle concave towards the opponent.

A Counter Thrust is one delivered at an opponent in the very act of making an attack. There is a certain psychic instant, when a man is just on the point of launching an attack, when he momentarily seems to lose the power to parry or even move and he will also often at this moment expose some part of his person which he expects instantly to recover by lunging. A Counter Thrust is delivered by the opponent at this critical moment. It is a Direct Lunge at the point selected and depends for its effect on the momentary torpor of the victim. Counter Thrust can be used to good effect against beginners who usually show quite clearly the moment when they will start a lunge. Just how they show it, I am unable to describe, but close observation will reveal it to most men. It is more felt than seen.

A Time Thrust is one delivered at the moment your opponent makes some move, as in changing from a high to a low guard or in executing a poor or slow feint. When an opening is given by such a move, lunge at once. Example: Expose your lower arm by raising your forearm from the elbow, your opponent will probably poke at it; the instant he starts to lower his hand to do so, extend your arm vigorously with the hand high and lunge at the shoulder.

Call the attention of the men to these preceding thrusts and have them practice in using them.

The Counter Thrust cannot be taught, it is simply to be suggested and those in the troop who have the soul of fencers will apprehend it.

Lesson 15.

The theory of feints. Various attacks.

A Feint is a threat such that the adversary must change either the position of his hand by a parry, or the position of his body by a retreat. To gain this result, the point of the man making the feint should approach nearer the spot threatened, than the sword of the defender is near to the threatening blade. Or, the feint must be made so suddenly, that it gains a start in time, sufficient to counteract the actual disparity in relative distance. A feint which does not conform to one or the other of the above requirements is useless and dangerous, it is apt to expose some part of the user's person to a Time Thrust.

Attacks using feints, either One-Twos or the One-Two-Threes, should be so combined that they will put the man on the defense at the greatest disadvantage. That is, a feint should be such, that the parrier must stop his blade and move it in the opposite direction to parry the expected lunge, when he is using Direct Parries. When he is using Counter Parries the feint should be such as to enable the man to deceive the counter or to make the defender use a second awkward parry.

Example of an attack fulfilling the requirements against a Direct Parry: feint Outside High, lunge Inside Low. The man parrying should have to make a Right High Direct, stop the motion of his sword, and then a Left Low Direct.

Example of similar case with a poor feint and attack: feint Inside Low, attack Inside High. The man parrying would simply have to convert his Left Low Direct into a Left High Direct, thus always moving his sword in the same direction, or convert his Left Low Direct Parry into a Counter Parry Up in this case, also his sword continues in the same direction.

54

In both these latter cases there would be no stopping and, so to speak, retracing of the steps so far as the motion of the sword in the parry was concerned.

All parries should seek on their completion to find the feeble of the attacker's blade against the forte of their own.

There should always be a difference of cadence in feints and lunges. If a man makes his feints and lunges always in the same cadence, it is much easier to parry him, than one constantly changing the rhythm of his movements, now making a fast feint followed by a slower lunge, now one fast feint, one slow, and then a fast lunge and so on always changing the cadence.

Do not parry twice in the same way if it can possibly be avoided. Your opponent will frequently feint simply to see how you parry an attack and then make his real attack in the same way trusting that you parry as before. Consequently he will be able to deceive your parry and touch you. On the other hand, had you parried differently every time you would probably have stopped him and gotten a chance for a riposte, or at least would have given him nothing on which to base an attack. It is very easy to fall into the habit of always parrying certain attacks in a certain way. It is a fatal error. Needless to say you should always notice whether or not your opponent makes this blunder.

All men using this diary will have graduated from the Mounted Service School, hence they should know a considerable number of attacks. The following attacks are enumerated here, not because of particular merit, but simply with the idea of stimulating the memory and imagination of the students.

There are almost a limitless number of combinations of feints and lunges but it is thought that a few thoroughly mastered and accurately applied, are better than many used in a haphazard way without accuracy.

Attacks: One-Two.

Feint Inside High; if parried Direct, lunge Outside Low.

55

Feint Outside Low; if parried Direct, lunge Inside High. The first feint in this attack may also be for the outside of the elbow.

Feint Inside Low, lunge Outside High or Low according to whether the parry is Direct or Counter.

Feint Outside High, lunge for the underside of the forearm if the parry is too high, otherwise lunge Inside High or Low.

In the case of a Counter Parry Up, to your first feint, deceive by disengaging below, or by disengaging above, in the case of a Counter Parry Down. This last advice is very general, for when these two parries are taken from the tierce or carte guard the disengagement is at times reversed. Space here does not, however, permit of discussing these special cases.

Attacks One-Two-Threes:

Feint 1. Outside Low; 2. Inside Low. Whether the second parry is Left Direct or Counter Up, disengage above and lunge Inside High; this is a nice attack for instruction in One-Two-Threes. I have attained the best results by making the first feint vigorous and brief, the second one vigorous and slower so as to induce a strong parry.

Feint 1. Outside High; 2. Inside High close to the arm. This will usually draw a Counter Up; deceive and lunge Inside Low. If it draws Left High Direct disengage below and lunge at the same place.

Feint 1. Outside High; 2. Outside Low lunge Inside High. The disengagement for the lunge is the same whether second parry is Counter Up or Down or Right Low Direct. A One-Two-Three is simply a One-Two with a new disengagement and lunge added. In all attacks with feints it is best to cross from the inside to the outside or conversely at least once. And the best results are obtained with One-Twos by making the feints in the outside line most of the time.

It is my opinion that direct attacks, that is, lunges not preceded by feints, are not used often enough; if executed with vigor they frequently succeed.

Do not forget to attack your opponent's arm on every possible occasion; it worries him if nothing more and keeps him from planning attacks.

Lesson 16.

Various Expedients.

As soon as you engage make a fierce lunge usually at the face. It gives you a moral advantage and puts your adversary in a defensive frame of mind. Be careful that he does not do the same thing to you.

If you encounter a man who uses the Stop Thrust excessively whenever you attack, make a half lunge to draw his stop, then use either an Overbind or parry Right Low Direct as you advance and lunge in opposition to his belly. In the latter case the advance must be very quick.

When fencing a man smaller than yourself do not use binds; it shortens your reach and puts you on par with him. Let little men do most of the attacking, thus saving yourself and gaining your touches by stop, thrusts or ripostes.

If a man stands out of distance and retreats whenever you advance, either force him to the end of the mat, or slowly shorten your guard by drawing in your hand and thus gain your distance, while still letting him think you are beyond it. Do not be in too great a hurry to touch and hence take foolish risks.

Never parry a feint until you have to. Your opponent makes a feint just to draw a parry so require him to make a good one. This is more tiring on him and may give you an opening for a riposte or a Time Thrust.

Do not develop the skin of an elephant and be unable to feel touches. Always admit the least touch. When you find a man who will not, only fence with him before a judge.

In the fear that some may read this diary who are not graduates of the school, I beg to call their attention to the fact that it is a much condensed resume of the course, and that the graduates are better fencers than the requirements of this diary might indicate. Fencing is an art, of which the best elements perish when put on paper.

To repeat, this diary was compiled at the request of student officers who wanted something on which to base the instruction of the men of their troops. This instruction in the troops has for its object to develop by means of the gymnastic game of fencing, the desire and ability to thrust and thrust accurately in battle.

GEORGE S. PATTON, JR.,
2nd Lieut. 15th Cavalry,
Instructor in Fencing, M.S.S.

June 1, 1915

DALE STREET BOOKS

U. S. Army Military Academy, *Campaign in Poland 1939*

Adam Mickiewicz, *Pan Tadeusz*

Polish Ministry of Foreign Affairs, *German Occupation of Poland*

Polish Ministry of Foreign Affairs, *The Mass Extermination of Jews in German Occupied Poland: Note addressed to the Governments of the United Nations on December 10th, 1942, and other documents*

Polish Ministry of Information, *The German Fifth Column in Poland*

George S. Patton, Jr., *Diary of the Instructor in Swordsmanship*

_____ *Saber Exercise 1914*

Aleksandra M. Rohde, *Quick Study for Your Technician Class   Amateur Radio License*

_____ *Quick Study for Your General Class Amateur Radio License*

_____ *Quick Study for Your Extra Class Amateur Radio License*

_____ *Wargame to Win*

Secretary of State for Foreign Affairs, His Majesty's Government, *Negotiations with a Madman: Stopping a War in 1939*

The Slovak Council, *Should Great Britain Go to War--for Czechoslovakia?: An Appeal to British common sense--for the sake of World Peace*

Sir Ernest D. Swinton, *The Defence of Duffer's Drift*

Made in the USA
Lexington, KY
27 October 2016